Question

ENCYCLOPEDIA

Answer&

UNIVERSE

Question ENCYCLOPEDIA Answer& UNIVERSE

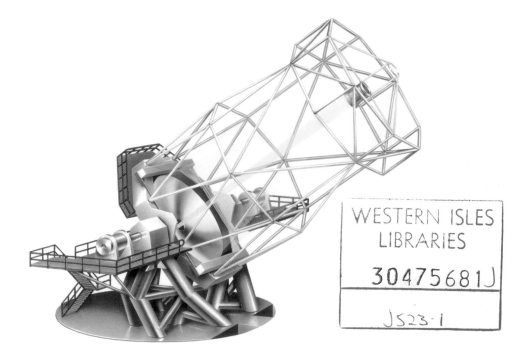

Brian Williams

Miles Kelly
PUBLISHING

First published in 2004 by Miles Kelly Publishing Ltd
Bardfield Centre Great Bardfield Essex CM7 4SL

2 4 6 8 10 9 7 5 3 1

British Library Cataloguing-in-Publication Data
A catalogue record for this book is available from the British Library

ISBN 1-84236-427-8

Printed in China

Publishing Director Anne Marshall
Senior Editor Jenni Rainford
Assistant Editor Teri Mort
Copy Editor Rosalind Beckman
Design Concept John Christopher
Designers Jo Brewer, Debbie Meekcoms
Cover Design Debbie Meekcoms
Picture Researcher Liberty Newton
Indexer Helen Snaith
Production Manager Estela Boulton
Colour Separation DPI Colour Digital Ltd

www.mileskelly.net
info@mileskelly.net

CONTENTS

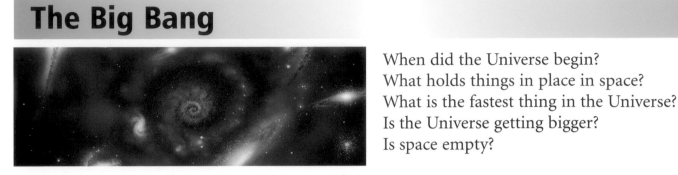

When did the Universe begin?
What holds things in place in space?
What is the fastest thing in the Universe?
Is the Universe getting bigger?
Is space empty?

What are twin stars?
Where is a star born?
Are all stars the same size?
How long do stars last?
Where does a star get its energy from?

When did people first see constellations?
Does everyone see the same stars?
What is Orion's Belt?
What is the Southern Cross?

Do all galaxies look the same?
Who realized there is more than one galaxy?
How big are galaxies?
Which galaxy do we live in?
What is dark matter?

What is the biggest object in the Universe?
Why did scientists put a telescope into space?
What are the most distant objects?
What is a supernova?
What goes into a black hole?

6   CONTENTS

Space Missions

What makes rockets the best engines for space flight?
How many people have stood on the Moon?
When did scientists land craft on the planet Mars?
Why do astronauts float in space?
How is a spacecraft launched?
Which spacecraft first explored the giant planets?

Searching the Sky

How does a telescope study the stars?
Why are telescopes put on mountain peaks?
What do radio telescopes detect?
Who first looked into space through a telescope?
Who made the first catalogue of the stars?

The Sun

What makes the Sun an unusual star?
What is inside the Sun?
Why does the Sun have spots?
What are solar flares?
What happens during a solar eclipse?

Earth in Space

How was the Earth formed?
What does the Earth look like from space?
Why do we have seasons?
How long is a year?
What makes the Earth unique?

The Moon

Can we see all the Moon from Earth?
How old is the Moon?
What is it like on the Moon?
What made the Moon's craters?
Why are there New and Full Moons?

Solar System

How many planets orbit the Sun?
Which planet is nearest the Sun?
Where could an astronaut fly through
a ring of snowballs?
What are the biggest planets made of?
Do any other stars have planets?
Which planets have been explored by spacecraft?

The Inner Planets

What are the inner planets made of?
Why is Mars called the red planet?
Which planet looks most like the Moon?
Could you see the stars from Venus?
Which planet is the hottest?
Which planet spins strangely?

The Outer Planets

What is the biggest planet made of?
Which planets have rings?
Which planet has the most satellites?
Which planet may have had a near-miss?
Which are the windiest planets?
Which are the least known planets?

Rocks in Space

What is a shooting star?
Where is the biggest meteorite crater on Earth?
What are asteroids?
What are comets?
What happened when an asteroid struck the Earth?

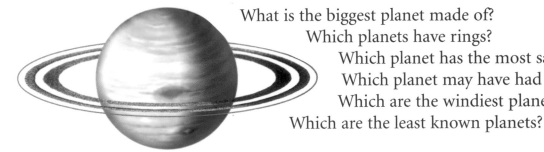

The Universe is where we live – all the stars we can see, and billions more besides. Scientists think the early Universe was very small, but still contained all the matter and all the energy there is today. And, to make it more amazing, scientists also think the original Universe lasted for less time than it takes to blink your eye. Then it began to grow. They call this theory the 'Big Bang'.

When did the Universe begin?

Many scientists believe that the Universe began between 13 and 18 billion years ago but no one is quite sure exactly when. What was there before remains a mystery. Some scientists think our Universe began as a 'bubble', which split off from another universe! Others think that in the beginning, all the matter in the Universe was squeezed into a tiny, incredibly hot, incredibly massive ball. When the ball began to get bigger, like a balloon being blown up, all the matter in the Universe started to explode outwards.

What holds things in place in space?

All the matter in the Universe – stars, planets, clouds of gas, tiny particles of dust – is held together by four invisible forces. These forces are gravity, electromagnetism, and two forms of nuclear force, strong and weak, which hold the particles of every atom together. Gravity is the attraction between all matter in the Universe. It keeps the Moon in orbit around the Earth, and the Earth in orbit around the Sun. The more matter a body has, the stronger its 'pull' on other bodies.

⬇ *This is the Horsehead Nebula, one of many 'star factories' in space where new stars are born.*

What is the fastest thing in the Universe?

Nothing in the Universe travels faster than light. Light is given off by stars, such as our Sun, and it travels through space at roughly 300,000 km/sec. Yet because the Universe is so large, even at this speed, light from the Sun takes more than eight minutes to reach us on Earth.

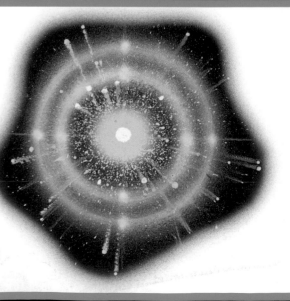

Measuring space and time

Light years and parsecs

Earth distances are measured in miles or kilometres, but these units are too small to be useful in space. Scientists measure the Universe in light-years and parsecs. Light is the fastest thing in the Universe, so by measuring in light-years scientists are able to get a better idea of such great distances. A light-year is the distance that light travels in one year – about ten million million km. A light-year is roughly 3.25 parsecs. Light from even the closest stars takes years to reach us. The nearest star is over four light-years away, so this means that when astronomers look at it through a telescope, they are actually looking back into the past – seeing the star as it was four years ago. Light from the most distant galaxies takes about 10,000 million years to reach us.

➡ *The Universe may go on expanding for ever. Or it may eventually stop and begin collapsing in on itself to possibly even start all over again.*

Is the Universe getting bigger?

Yes. Scientists can tell that groups of stars, known as galaxies, appear to be moving away from us. The galaxies themselves are not moving, but the space between them is stretching. By measuring how fast this distance is increasing, scientists can work out how long it has taken for everything to get where it is now. So they have a rough idea when the Big Bang set everything off.

← *Scientists can detect background radiation spread throughout space, probably left over from the Big Bang. In the 1920s, astronomer Edwin Hubble (1889–1953) discovered that there were other galaxies apart from our own Milky Way. The distance between Earth and each of these galaxies is increasing at unbelievable speeds.*

← *Scientists have calculated that the hot ball before the Big Bang must have swelled at a much faster rate than even the speed of light. The hot ball would have grown to the size of a galaxy within a fraction of a second!*

Is space empty?

Not really. Matter was created almost as soon as the Universe began. Space is littered with stars and gas clouds, made almost entirely of two elements: the gases hydrogen and helium. There are other elements too, such as iron, carbon and oxygen, but these are rare. The space between stars and planets is full of bits of space debris, including very tiny specks of dust and larger pieces of rock. Some of this space-dust forms clouds, called nebulae. These vast clouds of matter are the 'factories' inside which new stars and planets are made.

⬆ *Galaxies are giant groups of up to trillions of stars, and there may be as many as 20 trillion galaxies in the Universe.*

Telescopes and radio dishes

Early astronomers could only see stars visible with the unaided eye. Today, scientists use light-collecting telescopes and radio dishes that pick up radio and other waves to scan and photograph the most distant objects in outer space. Scientists depend mostly on these photographs to study space.

➡ *With the help of his sister Caroline, William Herschel (1738–1822) discovered Uranus in 1781. He later identified two of the moons of Uranus and Saturn.*

⬆ *Johannes Kepler (1571–1630) became the great Danish astronomer Tycho Brahe's assistant and took over his work when Brahe died.*

Amazing **Universe**

- In the first micro-seconds of the Universe, matter did not exist. There was just very hot space.

- Anti-matter is equal and opposite to matter: when the two collide, they eliminate one another.

- Hydrogen is the the most common element found in the Universe.

- Some scientists think there may be lots of 'parallel' universes, like a pack of cards – each 'card' separated by a fraction of time.

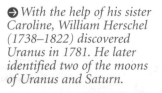

STARS

A star is a massive ball of hot hydrogen gas. To people on Earth, a star looks like a tiny pinpoint of light in the night sky. Stars look small because they are so far away. In fact, many stars are enormous, many times bigger than our Sun – our nearest star. The Sun glows fiercely because it is a star that is still hot and active. That is why we see it shining in the sky.

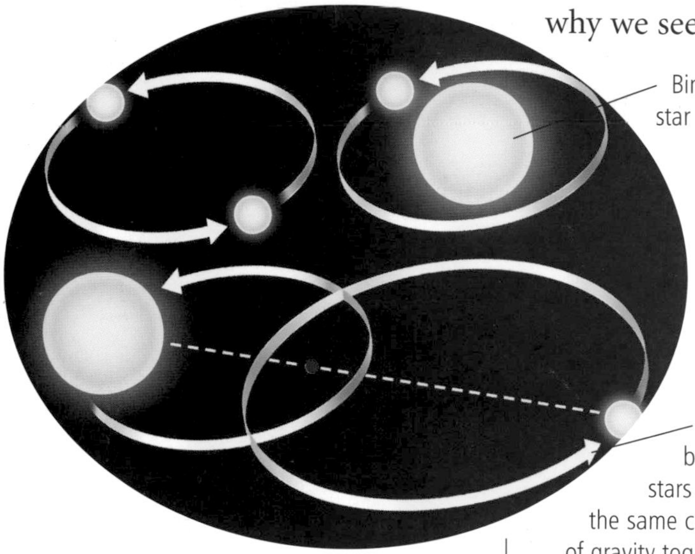

Binary system with one star larger than the other
True binary stars orbit the same centre of gravity together

About half the stars in our own galaxy are binary stars. They orbit around the same point, or centre of gravity.

Stars are born inside vast gas clouds. Some old stars die as exploding supernovae. Others swell up and become giants, which then fade and dim.

What are twin stars?

Some stars, like our Sun, are alone in space, but others, called binary stars, have companions or twins, which are held together by gravity. Eclipsing twin stars appear to 'dance' around each other in space. Binary stars move faster the closer together they are, but some may be so far apart that they take millions of years to orbit one another. When one star is hidden behind the other, its light is dimmed. When the star reappears, the pair of dancing stars shine brightly once more.

Where is a star born?

Stars are born inside giant dust and gas clouds called nebulae. There are nebulae in every galaxy across the Universe. Nebulae are 'star factories', as clouds of dust and gas shrink under the pull of gravity, the mass of matter becomes immensely hot and begins to give off energy as light and heat. A new star starts to shine.

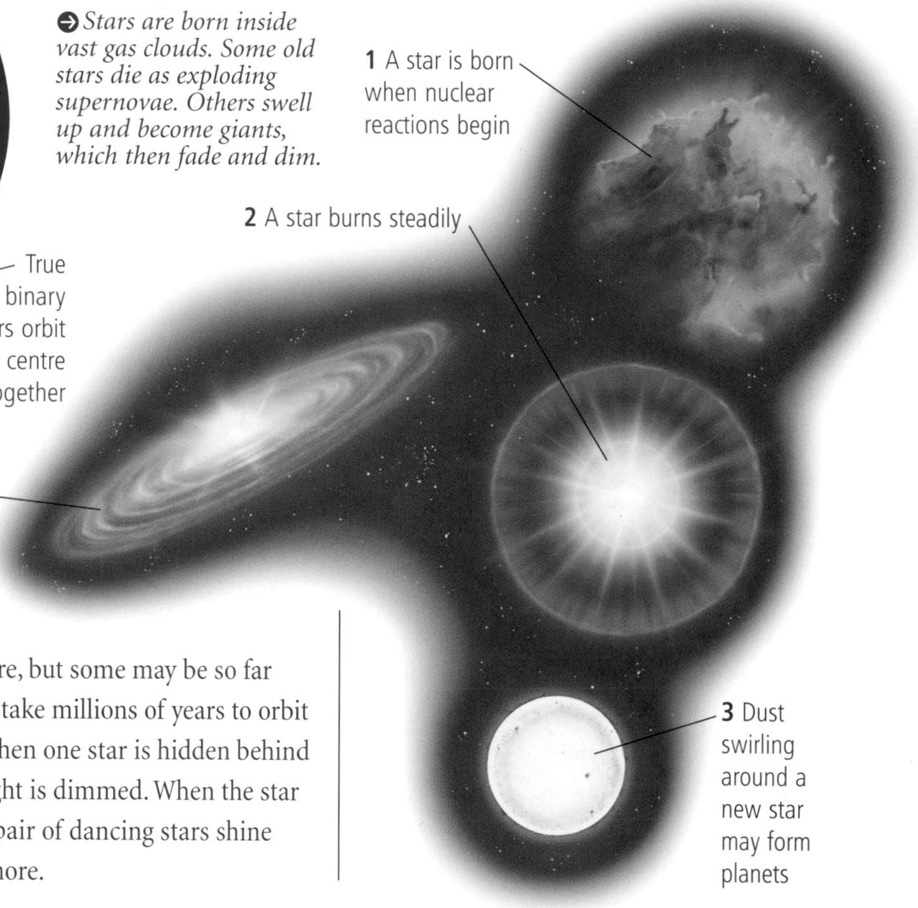

1 A star is born when nuclear reactions begin
2 A star burns steadily
3 Dust swirling around a new star may form planets
4 A nebula formed from cloud and dust

Starry facts

Countless stars

We know what stars are made of: 75 per cent hydrogen, 22 per cent helium and traces of other elements. But no one knows how many stars there are. Space seems to be full of stars and there are too many for one person to count in a lifetime! Star facts are mind-boggling. The Sun is more than 100 times bigger than the Earth, yet the Sun is a very ordinary star. Even huge stars look tiny in space because they are such vast distances away from us. The biggest stars are 700 times larger than our Sun.

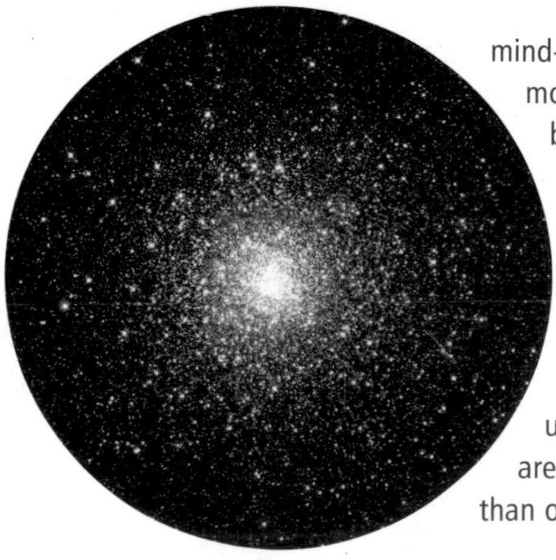

Are all stars the same size?

No, they vary in size and heat. Our Sun is a medium-sized hot yellow star. The biggest stars are called supergiants and there are many supergiant stars that are hundreds of times bigger than our Sun.

⬆ *This is a globular star cluster, made up of millions of stars of different ages and sizes.*

How long do stars last?

A star's lifetime may be up to millions of years. During their lives, stars burn up energy, sending out light and heat. Some grow into blue giants and explode as supernovae. Other smaller stars swell up as their fuel starts to run out and become vast glowing red giants. They then shrink into white dwarfs, which are very small, tightly compressed stars. White dwarfs are so small that they are hard to detect in the sky. The surface of a white dwarf can reach 8,000°C.

➡ *A cluster of ancient stars, or stellar swarm, is one of 147 such clusters in our galaxy. Every star in this cluster is older than our Sun.*

Where does a star get its energy from?

A star's energy comes from nuclear fusion, in which most of the hydrogen changes to helium, but enough hydrogen is left over to produce huge amounts of energy. The light from stars streams out across space in a range of colours (blue, orange-red, yellow and white).

⬇ *A star can shine for millions of years before it swells up to become a red giant, then shrinks to a small white dwarf.*

Star cloud

New star

Orange star

Red giant

White dwarf

⬅ *The largest telescopes can see about 100 billion galaxies. A galaxy can have up to 100 billion stars in it. Astronomers call this galaxy NGC 4214 and it is about 13 million light-years from us.*

Amazing **facts**

Brightest star: Sirius in the constellation Caris Majoris.
Smallest stars: Neutron stars are only 20 km across.
Nearest star (excluding the Sun): Proxima Centauri, 4.22 light-years away.

Star type	Temperature (°C)
Blue	up to 40,000
Blue-white	11,000
White	7,500
Yellow	6,000
Orange	5,000
Red	3,500

There are 88 'star patterns' visible in the night sky. These are the constellations. When the first astronomers in ancient Babylonia, Egypt, China and Greece began looking at the stars, they saw patterns and shapes, formed by stars that appear close together in the sky. They named each constellation after an animal or a character from myth and legend – such as Taurus (the bull) and Perseus (a Greek hero). Later, more constellations were discovered and given names, such as Telescopium (the telescope).

⬇️➡️ The star-groups seen in the Northern Hemisphere (below) are not the same as those seen south of the Equator, in the Southern Hemisphere (right). Stars are best seen on a clear, moonless night away from the glare of city lights.

When did people first see constellations?

Many constellations were first seen by astronomers living in China and Babylon more than 2,000 years ago. Stars fascinated early scientists, but the scientists had no telescopes, so could only name the star-groups that they could see with the unaided eye. Constellations are all different shapes and sizes, and it is not always easy to recognize the animal or object they are named after without a drawing showing an outline around the stars. Some star-groups have more than one name.

The ancient Greeks, called Orion the Hunter, but the ancient Egyptians called it the god Osiris.

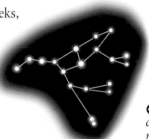

Does everyone see the same stars?

No. Different constellations can be seen in the Southern Hemisphere (south of the Equator) and in the Northern Hemisphere (north of the Equator). Many of the constellations were named before 2000 BC by astronomers in Babylonia. By AD 150, the Greek scientist Ptolemy was able to list 48. No new ones were added until European explorers sailed to the Southern Hemisphere and saw stars that are invisible to people in the Northern Hemisphere. Constellations are not easy to pick out because the night sky looks so crowded with stars. It helps to concentrate on the brightest stars.

◀ This is Ursa Major, the Great Bear, a constellation in the Northern Hemisphere. Its other names include the Plough and the Big Dipper.

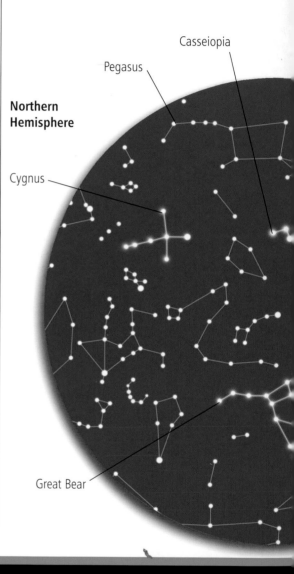

Northern Hemisphere

Casseiopia

Pegasus

Cygnus

Great Bear

Astrological **signs**

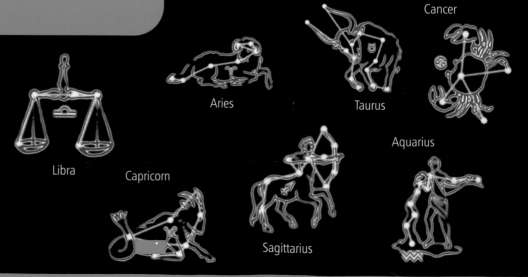

Stars and people
The Zodiac is a band of stars that seems to encircle the Earth, and in which the main planets are always found. The band is divided into 12 sections, known as the signs of the Zodiac, and each sign is named after a constellation. Early people thought that seasons and events on Earth were connected to the position of these stars. Astrologers still claim that people's lives are influenced by the zodiac and their 'birth-signs', but scientists disagree.

Cancer

Aries

Taurus

Aquarius

Libra

Capricorn

Sagittarius

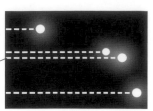

Southern Hemisphere

Same star pattern seen side on

Scorpion

Southern Cross

Great Dog

View from Earth

⬆ *Seen from the Earth, the stars making up the Southern Cross look the same distance away, but they are, in fact, scattered.*

What is Orion's Belt?

Orion's Belt is the name given to three bright stars in the constellation Orion (the Hunter). Orion can be seen from anywhere on Earth and because it is bright and easily seen, it makes a good star-guide. The Belt points in one direction to the star, Aldebaran, and in the other to the star, Sirius.

What is the Southern Cross?

The Southern Cross is the smallest of the constellations, but is well known because its stars are so bright. Some constellations contain very few bright stars and so are hard to see. Hydra, the Water Snake is the biggest constellation, but it is very dim and so incredibly difficult to spot.

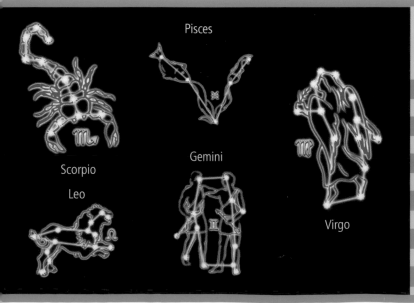

Pisces

Gemini

Scorpio

Leo

Virgo

Signs of the **Zodiac**

22 December–19 January	Capricorn, the Goat
20 January–18 February	Aquarius, the Water Carrier
19 February–20 March	Pisces, the Fish
21 March–19 April	Aries, the Ram
20 April–20 May	Taurus, the Bull
21 May–20 June	Gemini, the Twins
21 June–22 July	Cancer, the Crab
23 July–22 August	Leo, the Lion
23 August–22 September	Virgo, the Virgin
23 September–22 October	Libra, the Scales
23 October–21 November	Scorpio, the Scorpion
22 November–21 December	Sagittarius, the Archer

A galaxy is a vast group of stars, like a stellar city, which can contain as many as a trillion stars. Galaxies are found in clusters, some with fewer than 50 galaxies, others with hundreds. There are many millions of galaxies, each of which began as a cloud of gas when the Universe was formed and new stars are still being born inside them. As the Universe expands, the galaxies fly apart.

➜ *Hubble proved that the Universe was much larger than anyone had believed, by discovering that there are many other galaxies.*

Do all galaxies look the same?

No. The main shapes are spirals, ovals and irregular. Two kinds of galaxy look like whirling spirals with 'arms'. Spiral galaxies either have several arms of stars around a central core or, like our Milky Way galaxy, have arms that start from bars – this is a 'barred spiral'. Elliptical galaxies are oval or egg-shaped. Irregular galaxies have no set shape. Elliptical galaxies send out stars in all directions, like sparks from a huge firework.

Who realized there is more than one galaxy?

American astronomer Edwin Hubble first realized there was more than one galaxy in 1924. Until then, people thought there was just one mass of stars – making one very big galaxy. Hubble detected a winking variable star beyond the Milky Way. He realized that the Andromeda Nebula he was studying was not a gas cloud within our Milky Way galaxy, but was in fact another galaxy. All the stars that we can see with the unaided eye belong to our galaxy, but there are millions more beyond it.

⬇ *The four main kinds of galaxies are spiral, irregular, elliptical and barred spiral.*

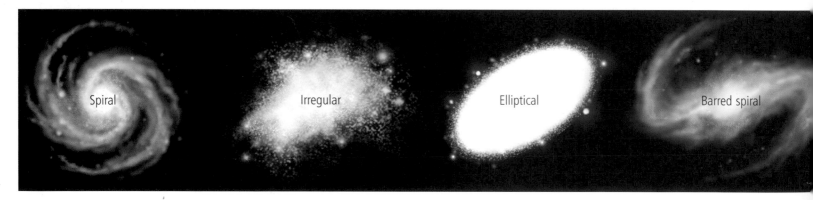

Spiral   Irregular   Elliptical   Barred spiral

Facts about our galaxy

Heavenly milk
The word 'galaxy' comes from the ancient Greek word for milk, *gala*. The Greeks saw a hazy belt in the night sky, which reminded them of a trail of spilt milk. They made up a story to explain that the heavenly milk had been spilt by the baby Heracles (Hercules). The galaxy came to be known as the 'road of milk', or Milky Way. The centre of the Milky Way is the core or nucleus of the galaxy, with a dense mass of stars.

The Sun is about halfway out from the centre, on one of the spiral arms of the galaxy.

Galaxies visible from Earth

The Large Magellanic Clouds	160,000 light-years away
The Small Magellanic Clouds	180,000 light-years away
The Andromeda Galaxy	2 million light-years away

What is dark matter?

Galaxies look like bright clouds of starry matter, but around them is a swirling mass of invisible 'dark matter'. Astronomers believe that nine-tenths of all the matter in the Universe is dark and know about the existence of it because its gravity pulls on stars and galaxies in the Universe. Dark matter could be the remains of ordinary matter, such as stars, which burnt out early in the life of the Universe.

⬆ *The Milky Way spins extremely quickly, moving the Sun and all the stars in it at up to 100 million km/h.*

Which galaxy do we live in?

Our galaxy is the Milky Way. There are about 200,000 million stars in the Milky Way galaxy, and one of them is our Sun. The Sun is moving around the galaxy, but in the last 200 million years it has only done this once as the galaxy is so big.

⬇ *This is an irregular galaxy, In ten days in 1995, the Hubble Space Telescope took photographs of almost 2,000 galaxies in one small area of sky.*

How big are galaxies?

Unbelievably vast. Even travelling at light-speed, a spacecraft would take 100,000 years to cross the Milky Way. A very ordinary galaxy contains a million stars, while the super-galaxies are giants with as many as a billion stars.

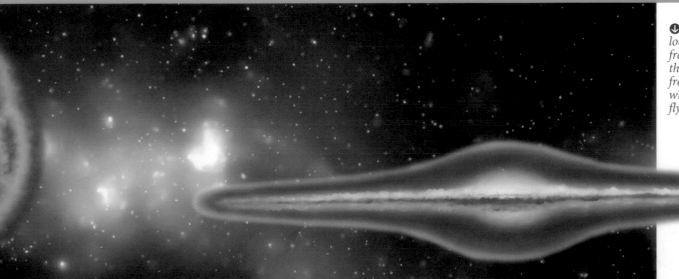

⬇ *The Milky Way looks different seen from 'above' (showing the spiral arms) and from sideways on, when it looks like a flying saucer (right).*

Our galaxy is amazingly big: two billion stars, 100,000 light-years across. But it is just one of millions of similar galaxies. As well as stars, there are other faraway objects in space: black holes, supernovae, nebulae and quasars. No one knows how many galaxies there are, all speeding away from us. The Big Bang expansion may go on forever. Or the Universe may slow down and contract, like a deflating balloon – a theory that scientists call the 'Big Crunch'.

What is the biggest object in the Universe?

The most gigantic object detected so far is a wall of galaxies, appropriately called the Great Wall. This stretch of stars is 500 million light-years long and 16 million light-years wide. However, size does not really matter in the Universe, because there are such a lot of giants out there.

Why did scientists put a telescope into space?

The Earth's atmosphere obscures our view of the stars, so the Hubble Space Telescope was launched in 1990 from the space shuttle, to give scientists a clearer view of space. It now circles in an orbit high above the Earth, where the view is unobscured. Hubble gave scientists their first unhazy view of the stars, and even though at first the telescope did not work as planned (it had to be repaired by astronauts), the results were astounding.

⊖ The Great Wall is a vast string of galaxies, like this spiral galaxy (photographed from the Hubble Space Telescope).

⊕ The Hubble Space Telescope weighs 11 tonnes and has a mirror 2.5 m across. When first launched in 1990, the mirror was the wrong shape and a replacement had to be taken up in 1994.

Nebulae and **neutron stars**

Clouds of dust and gas

Nebulae are huge clouds of dust and gas. These clouds are made mostly of hydrogen and helium – the raw materials of star-building, and it is inside nebulae that new stars are made. It is intensely cold inside a big nebula, only 10° above absolute zero. Clumps of gas are pulled together by gravity, and the more the atoms are squeezed, the warmer they become. The clumps do not all become new stars – some never get hot enough, but the bigger ones get hotter and hotter. We can see some nebulae through telescopes, some because they glow faintly and others because they reflect light from stars and so 'shine'. There are other nebulae that are dark, veiling the stars being born inside them.

⊖ The word nebula was once used to describe any patch of light in the night sky. Many nebulae are now galaxies instead.

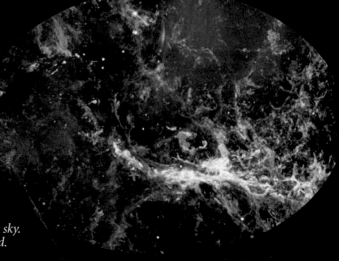

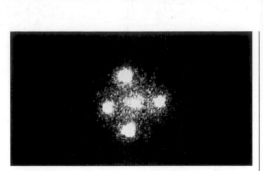

⬆ *Quasars send out vast amount of energy, in the form of radiation such as light, X-rays and radio waves. Studying these objects helps astronomers discover more about the early Universe, since the radiation from a quasar probably left it billions of years ago.*

What are the most distant objects?

Quasars, which look like stars, but actually are not. A quasar is much smaller than a galaxy (a mere light-year or two across), but up to a thousand times brighter. Quasars give off radio waves and would be invisible if they were not so incredibly luminous. Quasars are at least 10–13 billion light-years away from Earth, making them the most distant objects in the Universe.

Debris expands   Supernova explodes

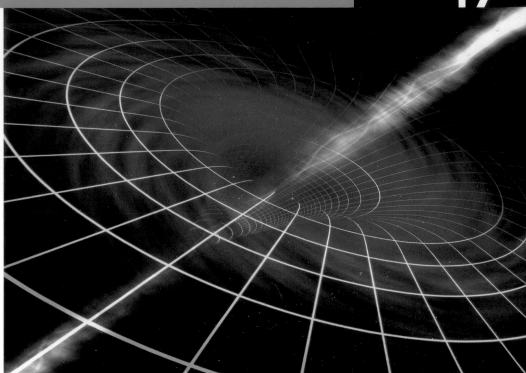

⬆ *This is an artist's impression of a black hole. Black holes suck up any type of matter. Some scientists think there may be a black hole at the heart of every galaxy.*

What is a supernova?

A supernova is a vast explosion of light, brighter than millions of suns, that happens when an old giant star collapses into itself. The collapse sets off a nuclear reaction and the explosion can be seen far across the Universe. In 1987, a supernova was visible from the Earth – a rare event.

⬅ *When a supernova explodes, star-debris is flung far out into space.*

What goes into a black hole?

Anything within reach. Nothing that goes into a black hole can come out. A black hole is all that is left of a collapsed star. It is invisible because it has such a strong gravitational pull that no matter and no light can escape from it. A black hole sucks up vast amounts of matter into an incredibly tiny space. To travel through interstellar space (between galaxies), astronauts in the future may have to use 'wormholes' – cosmic tunnels, which avoid black holes – if such tunnels exist.

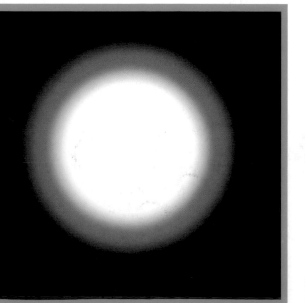

⬇ *A photo of the Horsehead Nebula, taken with a telescope on Earth. This nebula is in the constellaton Orion.*

Neutron stars

Neutron stars may be the smallest stars known, but they are incredibly dense. They form when a big star uses up all its fuel and collapses under its own gravity. All its matter gets squashed together, then the star explodes as a supernova and all that is left is a spinning core, called a neutron star. Neutron stars were first spotted as fast-spinning 'pulsars' in 1967.

➡ *A neutron star may be only 20 km across but it contains more matter than the Sun.*

Space missions involve travelling vast distances, either around or away from the Earth. To send people into space costs a lot of money and effort. So far, the only way to get into space is by using a big rocket. Rockets have sent people to the Moon and probes to the planets. Astronauts live and work in space stations, which orbit the Earth. For exploring the distant planets, a robot probe is best: it needs no air, water or food – and it never gets bored!

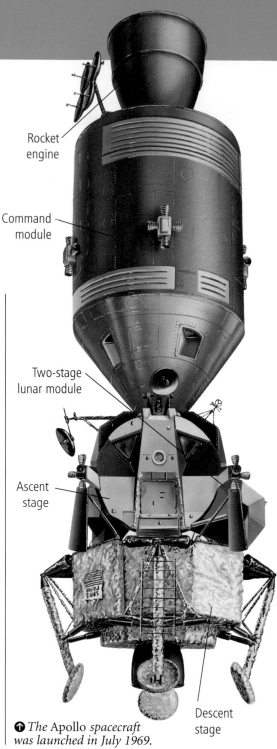

Rocket engine

Command module

Two-stage lunar module

Ascent stage

Descent stage

⊕ *The Apollo* spacecraft *was launched in July 1969.*

⊕ *The US Pathfinder landed on Mars with the roving vehicle* Sojourner. *The rover stopped working after three months on Mars.*

What makes rockets the best engines for space flight?

A rocket needs no air (unlike a jet engine) – indeed, air slows it down. Most rocket engines get their thrust from the reaction between a fuel, such as liquid hydrogen, and an oxidant (liquid oxygen), which allows the fuel to burn.

How many people have stood on the Moon?

Since the astronauts of *Apollo 11* first landed on the Moon in 1969, a total of 12 astronauts have stood on the Moon. From 1969 to 1972, the Americans sent seven Apollo missions to the Moon. One mission, *Apollo 13*, failed to land but returned safely after an explosion on board. The other six missions each landed two astronauts.

When did scientists land craft on the planet Mars?

Two US *Viking* spacecraft visited Mars in 1970–76. The craft orbited the planet and robot landers took samples of the soil and sent data and TV pictures back to Earth. In 1997, the US *Pathfinder* craft landed a rover called *Sojourner*, and in 2004 the US *Express Orbiter* craft sent two rovers to different sides of Mars to explore the surface.

Pioneers of **spaceflight**

Space activity
In 2003, *Voyager 1* became the first spacecraft to leave the Solar System. This small robot craft is one of the most remarkable pioneers of space flight. In 2004, the USA landed two golf-buggy sized rovers, *Spirit* and *Opportunity*, at different sites on Mars. Europe's *Mars Express Orbiter* craft surveyed the planet but could not spot the small rover *Beagle 2*, which disappeared after landing in December 2003.

⊕ *Unmanned robots can go on sending back data for years. The two* Voyagers *have been in space for more than 25 years.*

Message for aliens
So far no astronauts have travelled farther than the Moon. Since the Apollo missions ended, humans have been confined to flights in Earth orbit. Two unmanned probes called *Voyager 1* and *Voyager 2* left the Earth in 1977. They carried messages for any aliens that might find the tiny spacecraft somewhere in the vastness of space. The aim was to let any aliens know where in the Universe the small spacecraft had come from. Not every scientist thought this a good idea. What if the aliens are unfriendly? Fortunately, the chances of anyone finding the *Voyagers* lost in space is very remote!

Why do astronauts float in space?

Once in orbit, a spacecraft and the people inside it are freed from the full effects of Earth's gravity and so they feel weightless. Anything inside the spacecraft that is not fixed in place floats about. This takes a bit of getting used to, but most astronauts enjoy the experience of weightlessness. Exercises must be done to keep their muscles and bones in good shape.

An astronaut wearing a MMU (manned manoeuvring unit) can move safely about outside the spacecraft.

The Shuttle is lifted off the launch pad by the thrust of its three main engines and two booster rockets. It must reach a speed of 28,000 km/h to be able to go into orbit and not fall back down to Earth.

How is a spacecraft launched?

There are two kinds of launch systems for spacecraft: multi-stage rockets and reusable shuttles. The American space shuttle began its missions into orbit in 1981. It is launched with the aid of two solid-fuel rocket boosters, which fall off after two minutes and fall to the ground to be reused. After eight and a half minutes, the main fuel tank also drops away and the shuttle flies into orbit. On its return, the shuttle glows red-hot due to friction as it re-enters the atmosphere. It uses its wings to glide down to land.

Which spacecraft first explored the giant planets?

The US probe *Pioneer 11*, launched in 1973, flew past Jupiter and then on to Saturn in 1979 before heading out towards the edge of the Solar System. A later US space probe called *Voyager 2* flew past Jupiter in 1979, Uranus in 1986 and Neptune in 1989. The *Galileo* spacecraft visited Jupiter in 1995. Some long-range probes will probably go on travelling through space for ever, far beyond the Solar System.

Key **dates**

1926 First liquid-fuelled rocket.
1957 First artificial satellite launched by Russians: *Sputnik 1*.
1958 First US satellite: *Explorer 1*.
1961 First person in space: Russia's Yuri Gagarin.
1965 Russian *Venera* spacecraft hits Venus.
1965 First 'space walk' in orbit by Russia's Aleksei Leonov.

Valentina Tereshkova became the first woman cosmonaut in 1963.

1969 America lands two *Apollo 11* astronauts on the Moon.
1970 Russian *Venera 7* soft-lands on Venus.
1971 Russian *Salyut* is first space station in orbit.
1976 Two US *Viking* robot craft land on Mars.
1977 *Voyager 1* and *Voyager 2* probes leave Earth for the distant planets.
1981 First flight of US Space Shuttle – two are later lost in accidents.
1997 *Sojourner* rover explores Mars.
2003 *Voyager 7* enters 'interstellar space'.
2004 *Spirit* and *Opportunity* explore Mars.

The astronomers of the ancient world had no telescopes, but had to rely on their eyes to observe the stars, and on mathematics to try and make sense of what they could see. They named five of the nine planets and gave names to many stars. The use of the telescope in the 1600s revolutionized the science of star-gazing. For the first time, scientists could see details such as the craters on the Moon.

Why are telescopes put on mountain peaks?

Optical telescopes need a clear view of the night sky but the air above cities is just too 'fogged up' by air pollution, heat, gases and bright lights. Therefore telescopes are sited in observatories on high mountain peaks, where the air is thinner and clearer. Stars are best viewed from space.

⬆ *Astronomers use large telescopes like this one, located at the Kitt Peak National Observatory in Arizona, USA, to study the night sky. With such powerful lenses, experts are able to see and study stars that are too far away for us to see with the naked eye.*

How does a telescope study the stars?

Early telescopes were refracting (light-bending) telescopes, with a lens to collect light. In 1671, the English scientist Sir Isaac Newton built a telescope that had a mirror to collect light – this was the first reflecting telescope. Today, most optical (light-collecting) telescopes used by astronomers are reflectors, linked to computers that enhance the images of distant objects. Optical telescopes are still in use, even in the era of radio telescopes and space probes.

Telescope moves around to capture the best image

Main mirror to catch light from distant objects

Axle tilts the telescope

Secondary mirror

Platform for observation

Mount swings around

⬅ *The largest telescopes can see about 100 billion galaxies. Most modern optical telescopes are reflectors, and the bigger the mirror, the more light is collected. The same goes for radio dishes – big ones or lots of little ones see furthest.*

Seeing stars

Famous telescopes
The Hale Observatories on Mount Wilson and Mount Palomar in California, USA, has a 5-m reflector. Even bigger is the 6-m reflector at Zelenchukskaya in Russia.

Jodrell Bank in Cheshire, England has a 76-m diameter radio-dish.

The biggest optical telescope is the Keck telescope in Hawaii, which has 36 mirrors forming a light-collector 10 m across.

The world's biggest radio telescope is the Very Large Array (VLA) in New Mexico, USA. This multi-dish instrument has 27 dishes, each measuring 25 m across.

Effelsberg Radio Observatory in Germany has a 100-m dish.

➡ *Telescopes have come a long way since they were first used in the 1600s. People can now enjoy space observation at home with the use of personal telescopes.*

Who made the first catalogue of the stars?

A Greek named Hipparchus, who lived over 2,000 years ago. He was the first to notice that stars change their position in the night sky (this is called the precession of the equinoxes). Hipparchus made a list of the stars, showing their brightness and position. Hipparchus' writings about astronomy were lost, but his ideas were preserved by later astronomers such as Ptolemy.

What do radio telescopes detect?

Radio telescopes do not collect light, but pick up different forms of radiation (rays) from stars, such as radio waves and X-rays. Such telescopes can detect these rays, invisible to the eye, which can reveal, for example, the magnetic field around a planet or allow us to see through clouds of space dust.

⊙ *Radio telescopes have large dish antennae to collect rays reaching the Earth from distant space objects. Radio telescopes are linked to an array of other dishes, which together provide a clearer picture of space.*

⊙ *Hipparchus recorded the stars he could see with the naked eye – he had no telescope.*

Who first looked into space through a telescope?

The first scientist to use a telescope or 'spyglass' to look at the heavens was the Italian Galileo Galilei about 1609. With a telescope he had made himself, he saw four moons circling the planet Jupiter and also got the first close-up view of the craters on the Moon.

⊙ *Galileo made his own telescope. What he saw astonished scientists of the day.*

Key dates

1300s BC	Chinese astronomers map the constellations.
100 BC	Hipparchus makes a catalogue of stars.
500 BC	Pythagoras states that the Earth is round.
250 BC	Aristarchus proves that the Sun must be farther away from us than the Moon.
1540s	Nicolaus Copernicus demonstrates that the Earth moves around the Sun, not the other way round.
1608	Hans Lippershey of the Netherlands uses a telescope, though others probably invented it before him.
1609–10	Galileo makes a telescope to look at the skies and finds that the Sun has spots.

1668 Isaac Newton makes the first reflecting telescope, though the idea was suggested five years earlier by Scottish scientist James Gregory.

⊙ *Polish astronomer Nicolaus Copernicus's theories were so shocking to the people of the day that it was more than 100 years before his theories became widely accepted.*

The Sun is the centre of the Solar System. It is a star like the millions of other stars in the Universe. It is the 'offspring' of an older, bigger star, which, after it blew up, left clouds of gas behind. The Sun is a nuclear furnace inside, which hydrogen atoms are turned into helium – crushed by the enormous pressures. During this nuclear reaction, vast amounts of energy are created.

The chromosphere is a layer of gas. Bursts of heat-light energy called spicules flame through it

What makes the Sun an unusual star?

Only the fact that it is nearer to us than any other star – only 150 million km away. In all other respects, the Sun is a very ordinary star. It is middle-sized and middle-aged. But without the Sun, the Earth would be a dark, cold, lifeless world. You should never look at the Sun directly as its intense brightness could damage your eyes.

What is inside the Sun?

The Sun is not solid, but a very dense mass of gas. It has an outer surface called the photosphere and an inner layer known as the convection zone, and below that is the hottest part of the Sun – the centre or core, where the nuclear reactions take place. Energy moves from the core, through the many layers, such as the chromosphere and photosphere, to reach the surface and out into space. Without solar energy, the Earth would be lifeless.

The Sun's outer 'skin' is the corona, a halo-like layer of boiled-off gases

➔ *This cutaway of the Sun shows its different parts. The energy that is created inside the core takes ten million years to pass through its many layers and reach the surface.*

Giant tongues of hot gas, known as prominences, burst out from the chromosphere

Sun **worship**

The Sun's importance
Ancient people did not know what the Sun was, but they knew how important its warmth and light were to life. The ancient Egyptians, Greeks and Mayan people, among others, thought of the Sun as a god. They made up stories about the gods to explain the movement of the Sun across the sky. They were alarmed when there was an eclipse of the Sun, fearing that the Sun god must be angry. People also used the Sun as a means of telling

the time and making calendars. Stonehenge, a ring of 4,000-year-old stones in England, is a Sun calendar that indicates the time from the shadows cast by the stones. The Aztecs of Mexico sacrificed human victims to the Sun god, believing it would win his favour and therefore ensure the world's survival.

➔ *The Ancient Egyptians believed their Sun god Ra sailed a boat in the sky from east to west every day.*

The photosphere is a mass of hot gas, radiating heat and light into space

Radiating zone

The core of the Sun reaches 15 million°C

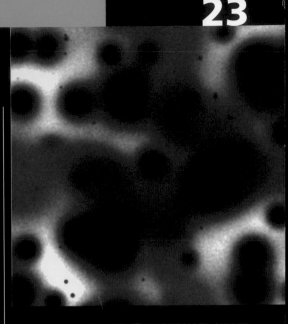
→ *Sunspots look darker because they are cooler than the rest of the Sun's surface.*

Why does the Sun have spots?

The photosphere or surface of the Sun is covered in dark blotches – sunspots – which are caused by changes in the Sun's magnetic field. They can be up to thousands of kilometres across. The number of sunspots we see varies from anything up to 100, over an 11-year cycle.

What are solar flares?

There are sometimes storms on the Sun, which send bursts of hot gas, called solar flares, into space. They shoot out light, heat and cosmic rays far beyond the Sun's atmosphere or chromosphere, and can break up radio communications on Earth.

What happens during a solar eclipse?

A solar eclipse occurs when the Moon blocks out light from the Sun, causing a shadow to pass across the Earth. Usually, most places on Earth see only a partial eclipse, but when the disc of the Moon blots out the Sun completely, day turns to night for about seven minutes. The Sun's corona can then be seen from Earth.

⬇ *Solar flares contain vast bursts of energy and coil out 100,000 km into space.*

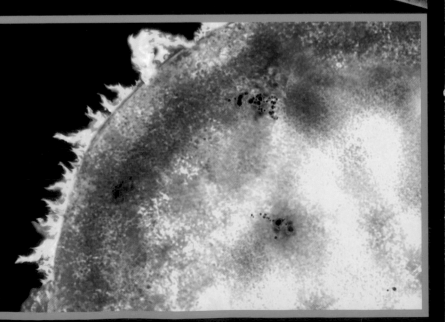

Amazing **Sun facts**

- Sunlight takes 8 mins 20 sec to reach us.

- The Sun's diameter is about 1,392,000 km – that's more than 100 times bigger than the Earth.

- The Sun is 400 times farther away from us than the Moon.

- The Sun is thought to be 4.6 billion years old, about the same age as the Earth.

- 98.8 per cent of all matter in the Solar System is in the Sun.

- The temperature at the surface of the Sun is about 5,500°C.

- The temperature at the core is much hotter, about 15 million°C.

The Earth is the planet we know best, but the first time we got a complete view of it was in 1968, when the *Apollo 8* astronauts flew around the Moon and saw the Earth floating in space. The Earth is just one of nine planets orbiting the Sun, all held in place by the Sun's massive gravity pull. Our world is a rocky ball, not quite round, with a belt of air around it like a protective blanket.

1 Dust and gas

2 Fiery Earth cools. Surface forms a crust

3 Gases and water vapour form the atmosphere

How was the Earth formed?

Scientists believe that the Earth began as a cloud of gas and dust, whirling around a new star – the Sun – before gravity forced the gas and dust together into a red-hot ball. Over millions of years it cooled and a rocky crust began to form. An atmosphere was formed from poisonous gases, such as methane, hydrogen and ammonia, which had risen from volcanoes on the surface of the Earth. Over billions of years, water vapour fell as rain from the clouds and the oceans began to form inside basins in the Earth's crust. The remaining landmasses formed the continents.

➲ *It took about 4.5 billion years for the Earth to form as it is now.*

4 Oceans and landmasses are formed

➲ *In the early stages of the Earth's formation lumps of rock called planetesimals formed from dust whirling around the Sun. Pulled together by their gravity, the planetesimals then formed the Earth and other planets.*

What does the Earth look like from space?

It is a beautiful blue-and-white globe, with patches of green and brown. Until about 500 years ago, most people were taught to believe that the Earth was flat. It is, in fact, round, though not a perfect sphere. It has a bulge around its centre, the Equator, and the poles are slightly flattened.

Where **are we?**

➲ *This is how Copernicus realized the Universe must work – with the Sun at the centre of the Universe. Earlier scientists had believed the theory of Ptolemy, a Greek living in Egypt, that the Earth was at the centre of the Universe.*

Plotting our position in the Universe

Until the 1500s most people thought the Earth was the fixed centre of the Universe. They believed the Sun and the other known planets moved around the Earth in a series of spheres. A Polish scientist named Nicolaus Copernicus (1473–1543) made the startling suggestion that the Sun was at the centre of the Universe, and that the Earth moved around the Sun, along with the other planets.

In 1762, two astronomers, Jacques Cassini and Jean Richer, worked out fairly accurately how far the Earth was from the Sun (between 147 and 152 million km), by first measuring the distance to Mars and then using geometry. Today, scientists measure the distance between planets by firing laser and radar beams at them.

Why do we have seasons?

As the Earth moves around the Sun, different parts of the Earth get more or less light and warmth from the Sun, making the different seasons. The Earth spins on its own axis (an imaginary line through the planet from pole to pole) and is tilted 23° out of vertical. The closer one side gets to the Sun the warmer it is and is therefore summer – less warmth means winter, in-between are spring and autumn.

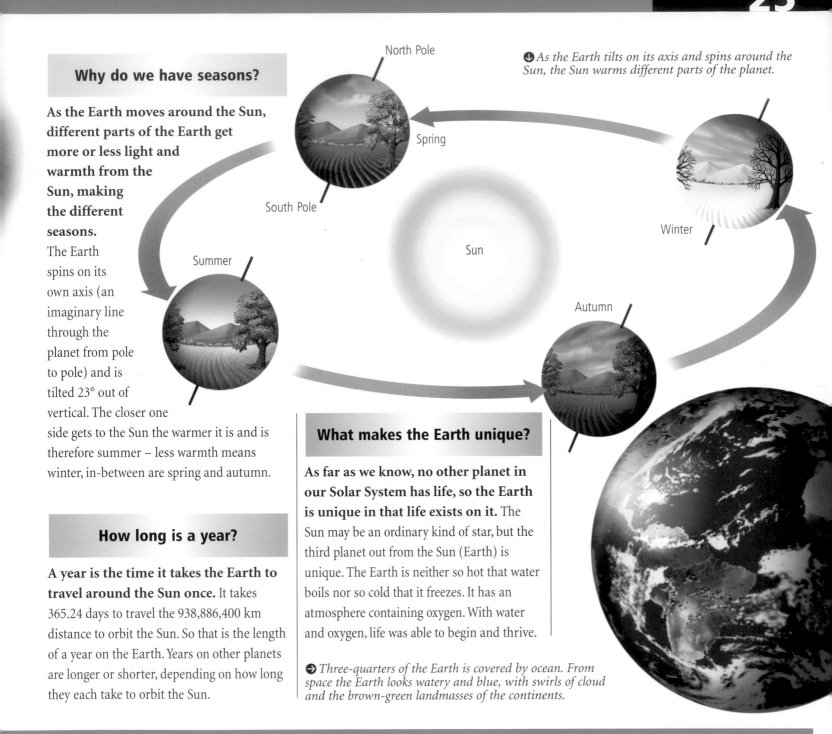

North Pole

Spring

South Pole

Summer

Sun

Winter

Autumn

⬇ *As the Earth tilts on its axis and spins around the Sun, the Sun warms different parts of the planet.*

How long is a year?

A year is the time it takes the Earth to travel around the Sun once. It takes 365.24 days to travel the 938,886,400 km distance to orbit the Sun. So that is the length of a year on the Earth. Years on other planets are longer or shorter, depending on how long they each take to orbit the Sun.

What makes the Earth unique?

As far as we know, no other planet in our Solar System has life, so the Earth is unique in that life exists on it. The Sun may be an ordinary kind of star, but the third planet out from the Sun (Earth) is unique. The Earth is neither so hot that water boils nor so cold that it freezes. It has an atmosphere containing oxygen. With water and oxygen, life was able to begin and thrive.

➡ *Three-quarters of the Earth is covered by ocean. From space the Earth looks watery and blue, with swirls of cloud and the brown-green landmasses of the continents.*

Earth layers

Scientists call planet Earth the geosphere. The outer rocky part on which we live is the biosphere. Surrounding this is the atmosphere, in layers. The inside of the Earth is also in layers. At the centre is a solid inner core made of an alloy of nickel and iron squeezed together under massive pressure. The rocks surrounding the core are hot and liquid.

Earth **facts**

Solar day	24 hrs
Spins on axis	23 hrs 56 mins and 4 sec
Orbits Sun (sidereal period)	365 days 6 hrs 9 mins and 10 sec
Velocity in orbit	29.8 km/sec
Rotation velocity at Equator	0.5 km/sec
Escape velocity	11.2 km/sec

⬅ *This telescope was used by the astronomer Sir William Herschel (1738–1822). His most famous discovery was the planet Uranus, in 1781. He was the first scientist to make a thorough study of the night sky.*

The Moon is the Earth's only satellite. Other planets have many more moons. Our Moon is the closest body to us in space, and has always fascinated people. Like the Sun, the Moon was thought by some ancient peoples to be a god. The Moon was probably hot when young, with volcanoes, but it has cooled down much faster than the Earth. It has also lost whatever atmosphere it may once have had.

People once thought the flat areas of the Moon were seas or dried-up seabeds. They gave them the Latin name mare *(sea). They are in fact plains of very old volcanic lava.*

The near side of the Moon, pock-marked with craters

How old is the Moon?

The Moon may be a little younger than the Earth, perhaps 4.5 billion years old. One theory about its birth is that a rocky mini-planet smashed into the Earth. Bits of rock from the collision were hurled into space and came together to form the Moon, which was then trapped in orbit by Earth's gravity.

The Moon may have been formed when a smaller, newly-formed planet collided with the Earth early on in the formation of the Solar System.

Can we see all the Moon from Earth?

No. The Moon orbits the Earth in the same time (27.3 days) as it takes for it to rotate once on its axis. This oddity keeps one side always facing away from us. Until the *Apollo 9* spacecraft flew around the Moon in 1968, no one had ever seen the far side, which actually turned out to look much the same as the near side.

What is it like on the Moon?

The Moon is very quiet and very still. It has no atmosphere, so there is no wind. It has no surface water either. The surface is dry and dusty. There are ancient craters measuring up to 1,000 km across and mountains as high as the highest mountains on Earth, such as Mount Everest, which measures 8,863 m above sea level.

Moon **facts**

Our Moon
The Moon has roughly the same surface area as the continent of Africa. It is about a quarter of the size of the Earth and has about one-sixth the gravity. This means that astronauts on the Moon weigh a sixth of what they weigh on Earth. So they can jump six times higher – although spacesuits makes acrobatics difficult and dangerous.

From the surface of the Moon, the Earth looks close, but is in fact 384,000 km away.

An astronaut's footprint left on the Moon will remain there for centuries because there is no wind or erosion to disturb it.

⊕ When US astronauts raised the Stars and Stripes flag on the Moon, it had to be stiffened to 'fly' because there is no air on the Moon to move it.

Why are there New and Full Moons?

The Moon is moving around the Earth and because one side of the Moon is always in sunlight, we see different amounts of the lit half as it moves. This means that the Moon seems to change shape during each month. These changes are known as the phases of the Moon. At New Moon, we cannot see any of the lit half. After a week, we can see about half a Moon (the Moon is waxing or getting bigger), and at Full Moon, we can see the whole lit disc. Then we see less of the Moon (it is waning) until by the last quarter, we again see only half the lit part, and finally a sliver of the 'old moon'.

What made the Moon's craters?

The craters on the Moon were created by space-rocks (meteors) smashing into it. The Moon is covered with craters, as if someone had been throwing stones into a ball of soft clay. The Moon has no atmosphere to burn up incoming space debris, and no weather to wear away the craters.

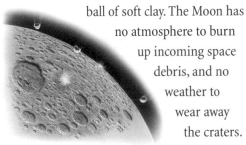

⊕ Craters on the Moon are as well-defined as when they were first made, because the Moon has no wind or rain to smooth them away.

⊕ The changes from New to Full Moon and back again are called the phases of the Moon. The full cycle from New to Full and back to New again takes one month.

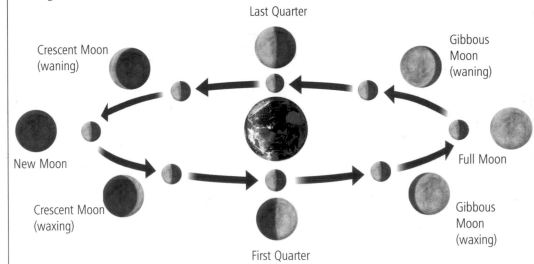

Last Quarter

Crescent Moon (waning)

Gibbous Moon (waning)

New Moon

Full Moon

Crescent Moon (waxing)

Gibbous Moon (waxing)

First Quarter

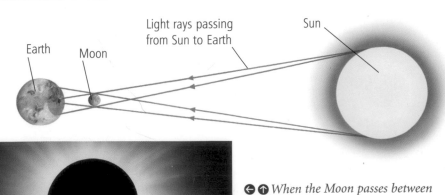

Light rays passing from Sun to Earth

Sun

Earth   Moon

◐⊕ When the Moon passes between the Earth and the Sun, it causes a solar eclipse, that is, it blocks out the light from the Sun momentarily.

Moon **facts**

Distance from Earth	384,399 km (average)
Diameter	3,476 km
Biggest crater (far side)	South Pole-Aitken – 2,500 km across and 12,000 m deep
Biggest crater (visible)	Bailly Crater – 295 km across and 4,250 m deep
Highest mountains	8,000 m near the Korolev Basin (far side)
Length of day	20 days 12 hrs and 44 mins
Mass	0.012 that of the Earth
Density	0.061 that of the Earth

The Solar System is the name for the 'family' of planets that orbit the Sun. In addition to the planets, there are millions of much smaller bodies travelling through space around the Sun. These include minor planets or asteroids, and comets that sweep close to the Sun and then travel out far beyond the outer planets.

Sun

Earth

Moon

Mars

Venus

Mercury

Neptune

Pluto

Uranus

Saturn

Jupiter

⬆ *The planets orbit the Sun at different distances.*

How many planets orbit the Sun?

Nine planets orbit the Sun, including the Earth. They were formed from material which about 4,600 million years ago was spinning around the Sun. Mercury, Venus, Mars, Jupiter and Saturn can be seen with the naked eye because they shine brightly with reflected sunlight. You need a telescope to see Uranus, Neptune and tiny Pluto.

Which planet is nearest the Sun?

Mercury is the planet closest to the Sun. It orbits the Sun at a distance of 58 million km. If you think of Mercury as one pace away from the Sun, the Earth is two and a half paces away. Mercury moves very fast around the Sun. One day on Mercury is equivalent to 59 Earth days, and a year lasts only 88 Earth days.

Where could an astronaut fly through a ring of snowballs?

Around Saturn, the planet with the biggest set of rings in the Solar System. Saturn has thousands of rings, which from far away look solid. However, close-up, an astronaut would see millions of icy particles, like hailstones and small snowballs, whirling around the giant planet. Some of Saturn's smaller moons hurtle around near the edge of the rings – these have been called shepherd moons because, like sheepdogs chasing sheep, they seem to be keeping the smaller particles in their orbits.

⬅ *Twice during its orbit, Mercury gets very close to the Sun and speeds up so much that the Sun seems to go backwards in the sky.*

Planet **data**

Different worlds

The Sun's nine planets are the space worlds we know most about, even though it takes months or years to reach each of them by spacecraft because the Solar System is at least 20 billion km across. However, unmanned spacecraft have visited eight of the nine planets and actually landed on two of them.

Planet **record holders**

Hottest	Venus	462°C
Coldest	Pluto	Approximately −235°C
Fastest-moving	Mercury	172,000 km/h
Faintest	Pluto	Only visible through a telescope
Most dense	Earth	Five times denser than water

⬅ *The Sun's nine planets are seen here, accurate in terms of sequence and appearance, but not in terms of size.*

What are the biggest planets made of?

The four biggest planets – Jupiter, Saturn, Uranus and Neptune – are vast balls of gas. There are two kinds of planet – rocky and gassy. Although the gassy planets are much bigger than the Earth, they are actually not very dense.

Do any other stars have planets?

It was once thought that the Solar System was unique, but scientists have discovered other stars with planets orbiting them. The distant star Upsilon Andromedae (44 light-years away) has three planets circling it. One of them is four times bigger than Jupiter. About 20 planets have been found orbiting other stars. But this is the only other Solar System spotted so far.

Which planets have been explored by spacecraft?

Robot spacecraft have been sent from the Earth to fly past Mercury, Jupiter, Saturn, Uranus and Neptune. Spacecraft have already landed on Mars and Venus, and mapped these planets from orbit. The 'easiest' planet to explore is Mars – at least its atmosphere does not crush or melt spacecraft landing on its surface.

⬆ *The nine planets in our Solar System, in order from the Sun, are: Mercury, Venus, Earth, Mars, Jupiter, Saturn, Uranus, Neptune and Pluto*

The **planets**

Name	Discovered	Distance from Sun (million km)	Diameter (million km)
Mercury	Ancient times	58	4,878
Venus	Ancient times	108	12,104
Earth	–	150	12,756
Mars	Ancient times	228	6,790
Jupiter	Ancient times	778	142,980
Saturn	Ancient times	1,427	120,536
Uranus	1781	2,870	51,120
Neptune	1846	4,504	49,528
Pluto	1930	5,900*	2,300

Pluto has an unusual orbit, which at times brings it closer to the Sun than Neptune.

The four inner planets, which include the Earth, are comparatively small. The other three are Mercury, Venus and Mars. We know more about them than we do about the outer planets, because exploration by spacecraft is possible, even though a journey to Mars takes six months – so planetary exploration is a very patient business.

What are the inner planets made of?

The four inner planets are made of rock and have hard surfaces. Each one has an outer crust enclosing a mantle of sticky-hot, semi-melted rock with, in the middle, a core of iron and nickel. They are also referred to as terrestrial (Earth-like) planets. Each of the four inner planets has some kind of atmosphere – a layer of gas – although Mercury has very little atmosphere to protect against the heat of its neighbour, the Sun. However the similarities with Earth and the inner planets end there.

⊕ *Robot landers have photographed the barren surface of Mars.*

Why is Mars called the red planet?

Mars looks reddish because its rocks contain a lot of iron dust. This dust has been oxidized by the carbon dioxide gas in the Martian atmosphere. This chemical reaction has in effect turned Mars rusty.

⊖ *Mars has seasons and what are probably water-containing ice-caps. Rivers may have flowed across Mars millions of years ago.*

Which planet looks most like the Moon?

Mercury is a small rocky ball with craters all over the surface. It has hardly any atmosphere – all gases except traces of vaporized sodium are boiled off by the blazing heat of the nearby Sun. Without an atmosphere to burn up incoming debris, any rock flying through space towards the planet is able to impact on the surface – smashing new holes in the surface.

⊖ *Mercury is the second smallest of the planets, and closest to the Sun.*

Earth and Mars **compared**

Earth and Mars

Mars is a very different planet from Earth. Mars is 228 million km away from the Sun, compared to Earth's 150-million-km distance. Due to this larger distance, Mars takes 687 days to orbit the Sun, whereas Earth takes only 365. The mass of Mars is only one-tenth that of the Earth and its diameter of 6,790 km is only half that of Earth's (12,756 km). Nights on Mars are chilly – as cold as the poles on Earth. Winter on Mars is colder than on Earth.

Temperatures on Mars can plunge to –125°C, cold enough to freeze carbon dioxide gas in the atmosphere. There is no oxygen on Mars, so no human could live there without the use of a spacesuit. Earth has one moon but Mars has two moons, Deimos and Phobos.

However, there are also some similarities between these two planets. Like the Earth, Mars has canyons and volcanoes on its surface. Its longest canyon, Valles Marineris, could contain the Grand Canyon, in the USA.

⊕ *Mars is our nearest neighbour planet, and the world that most attracts scientists planning future space missions, perhaps even a manned landing on the planet.*

Could you see the stars from Venus?

No, because this planet has a thick atmosphere of poisonous gas clouds that blot out the Sun and stars. The sky looks red and the clouds are so thick that it is impossible to see the surface of Venus from Earth. Venus also has rainfall of acid and is altogether unwelcoming. No space probe landed there so far has kept working for more than an hour.

Which planet is the hottest?

Venus is the hottest – even hotter than Mercury. The temperature on Venus reaches 470°C, which is hot enough to melt some metals. Venus has an atmosphere of carbon dioxide, which traps the heat from the Sun like a blanket. It is like the 'greenhouse effect' on Earth, only worse.

Which planet spins strangely?

Venus spins in the opposite direction to Earth. Unlike Earth, which spins in an anti-clockwise direction, Venus spins clockwise. If it were not for the clouds, someone on Venus would see the Sun rise in the west, and set in the east. Venus also spins very slowly, only once every 243 Earth days. Venus is almost exactly the same size as Earth at 12,000 km across, but weighs one-fifth less.

⊕ *Venus is shrouded in clouds of sulphuric acid, which hide the surface.*

The highest mountain on Mars is called Olympus Mons and is three times higher than Mount Everest. In 1976, a photo taken by a Viking probe showed what some people claimed was a giant stone face on Mars. Later photos showed it was a rocky hill.

In the late 19th century, Italian astronomer Giovanni Schiaparelli thought he had found another similarity between Earth and Mars. Looking through a telescope, he thought he saw canals on Mars. This caused great excitement. Did this mean there were, or had been, Martians? However, later observations proved there are no canals and it is believed that what he actually saw might have been shifting sand trails or wind-blown markings.

➔ *Unlike Mars, the appearance of Earth is very varied. Water and land can be seen all over the planet, and the atmosphere contains clouds and gases.*

The outermost planets from the Sun include the four gas giants – Jupiter, Saturn, Uranus and Neptune. These planets are all much bigger than the Earth, yet apparently with no solid surfaces at all. Their rocky cores are buried within masses of liquid and slushy, frozen gas. The fifth outer planet, Pluto, with its companion moon Charon, is a ball of rock-hard ice.

Jupiter spins so fast that a day on Jupiter lasts only just under ten hours. The Great Red Spot is a violent whirling storm on the planet.

What is the biggest planet made of?

The biggest planet is Jupiter, but no spacecraft can land on it because there is no 'ground', it is just a whirling mass of gases, mostly hydrogen and helium. It spins faster than any other planet, so fast that the clouds in its atmosphere are whipped up into vast, swirling storms with winds of up to 500 km/h. The Great Red Spot visible on the surface of Jupiter is a huge storm, a giant gas-hurricane, which is as big as the size of two Earths.

Which planets have rings?

Jupiter, Saturn, Uranus and Neptune all have rings. Saturn's rings are the most brilliant, measuring 270,000 km from edge to edge. The rings are made of millions of blocks of ice whizzing around the planet. Saturn's rings can be seen from Earth through a telescope. When, in the 1980s, robot spacecraft flew close to Jupiter, Neptune and Uranus, their rings were seen for the first time.

Saturn's rings are one of the most spectacular sights in the Solar System.

Which planet has the most satellites?

Uranus has at least 21 moons (satellites). Saturn and Jupiter each have more than 18 moons – new tiny ones are still being discovered. Four of Jupiter's moons are bigger than Pluto. The biggest moon in the Solar System is Jupiter's moon Ganymede, which measures 5,276 km across. Saturn's biggest moon Titan is only a bit smaller than Ganymede. The planets with the least moons are Earth and Pluto, which only have one each.

Outer planet facts

Varied planets

The outer planets are very varied and different from our planet, Earth. Saturn's moon Titan is one of the few moons with an atmosphere. Its sky is a mass of yellowish clouds. Jupiter's moon, Europa, is interesting because it is covered by ice, and is very smooth. Could there be a cold, watery ocean underneath, maybe with some form of life in it? On Triton, the biggest of Uranus's 17 moons, it gets incredibly cold – as cold as Pluto.

Geysers on Triton shoot out plumes of frozen nitrogen gas. Neptune probably has a hard core and has violent storms raging on it. Uranus is calmer than Neptune, and probably cold inside as well as out.

Neptune and Uranus are gas giants, too. Neptune has a Great Dark Spot, similar to Jupiter's Great Red Spot, a whirling storm bigger than the Earth!

Which planet may have had a near-miss?

Uranus is tilted on its side, perhaps because of a space collision that could have almost destroyed it. Scientists think that a giant asteroid may have smashed into Uranus and knocked it sideways. Miranda, one of Uranus's moons, looks as if it was blasted into chunks and then stuck back together again by gravity.

Uranus

Which are the windiest planets?

Jupiter and Saturn are the windiest planets. Both spin so fast that all the gases in their atmosphere are whipped around at speeds of up to 500 km/h on Jupiter and even faster on Saturn, around 1,300 km/h – that is more than ten times faster than a hurricane on Earth!

Neptune

Which are the least known planets?

Hardly anything is known about Pluto and its moon-neighbour Charon. Both worlds are made mostly of ice with a thin nitrogen–methane atmosphere. Pictures taken by the Hubble Space Telescope show hazy markings and brighter areas around the poles. Pluto is the furthest planet from the Sun, and so takes 248 years to orbit the Sun, swinging out to a maximum 7.3 million-km distance away.

⊙ *Like Earth, Pluto only has one moon – Charon, visible from the surface of the planet. Pluto is the smallest of the planets.*

⬅ *Uranus and Neptune have rings, too. Both these blue-green worlds are shrouded in clouds of poisonous methane gas above a freezing chemical slush surface.*

Big and small
Jupiter is so big that 1,000 Earths could fit inside it. But the Sun is bigger: in fact 90 per cent of all the matter in the Solar System is contained in the Sun. Almost 900 Jupiters would fit into the Sun. Jupiter has the shortest day of all the planets. A day on Jupiter lasts just 9 hrs 55 mins.

➡ *The little Galileo space probe hit Jupiter's atmosphere in 1995. It lasted an hour in the stormy, freezing clouds before it was first crushed and then vaporized.*

Outer **planet facts**

Planet	Volume compared with Earth (Earth = 1)	Atmospheres
Jupiter	1,300	Thick atmosphere of gases, mainly hydrogen, with clouds of ammonia, sulphur and other chemicals
Saturn	766	Hydrogen and helium gases, and ammonia clouds
Uranus	63	Methane and other gases
Neptune	58	Methane and other gases
Pluto	0.0058	Nitrogen–methane

Travelling through space across the Solar System are other bodies, including asteroids, meteors and comets. They provide brilliant light-shows in the night sky from time to time, and also give scientists clues to the origins of the Universe.

⊙ *Shooting stars flash across the night sky as meteors burn up in the atmosphere.*

➲ *Asteroids sometimes stray close to the Earth, but most stay within the so-called asteroid belt, further out from the Sun. Comets travel far out across the Solar System, occasionally passing by the Earth.*

What are asteroids?

Asteroids are mini-planets that orbit the Sun in a 'belt' between Mars and Jupiter. Most big asteroids look like rugged chunks of rock, with small craters blasted by collisions with smaller space-particles. The biggest asteroid is called Ceres, and is about 930 km across.

What is a shooting star?

'Shooting stars' are the glowing tails of meteors, which heat up as they enter the Earth's atmosphere. Millions of tiny lumps of metal or rock called meteoroids whizz through space, orbiting the Sun. As they hit the thick atmosphere around the Earth – about 90 km away from the Earth's surface – they heat up and for a second or two leave glowing trails behind them. They flash through the sky like brilliant firework displays.

Where is the biggest meteorite crater on Earth?

The biggest hole made by a meteorite is Meteor Crater in Arizona, USA – it is more than 1,700 m across and nearly 200 m deep. Occasionally meteors are big enough to hurtle through the atmosphere and smash into the ground. The charred rock that remains is a meteorite.

➲ *The biggest meteorites are massive chunks of rock, but few this big ever reach the ground.*

Spot the comet

Comets and meteorites

Halley's Comet can be seen from Earth as it passes the Sun every 77 years, but there are other comets that can be seen more often. Comet Encke returns every three years, and Comet Grigg-Skjellerup every four years. Comet Hale Bopp was spotted by two astronomers on the same night in 1995, so it was named after both of them. Something very big, either a large meteorite or the fragments of a comet, hit the Earth's atmosphere in 1908.

It exploded before smashing into a remote region of Siberia, Russia. The explosion was heard hundreds of kilometres away and forest trees were flattened over a wide area. The Hoba meteorite, found in 1920, is big enough for an entire football team to sit on it. A smaller meteorite, weighing 44 kg, landed in Leicestershire, England, in 1965.

➲ *Meteors pass by the Earth often and a large one could collide with the Earth at any time. However, most are very small and burn up as they enter the atmosphere.*

What are comets?

Comets are chunks of ice filled with dust and rock that orbit the Sun, just like planets. However, comets travel much farther out into distant space, often to the outer reaches of the Solar System, so comets can take up to thousands of years to make one orbit of the Sun. As a comet nears the Sun's heat, the ice core warms up and throws out a glowing tail that can be millions of kilometres long. It is a spectacular sight.

⬇ Small asteroids are burnt up by the Earth's atmosphere every day. The chances of a big one colliding with us and destroying the Earth, like in this illustration, are remote.

⬆ Comets are Solar System wanderers, which return on schedule. This photograph of Halley's Comet was taken when it last came close to Earth in 1986. The comet comes back close to Earth, within visible range, roughly every 77 years (see panel below).

What happened when an asteroid struck the Earth?

Many scientists believe that the effects of an asteroid collison about 65 million years ago may have been responsible for wiping out the dinosaurs. An impact crater, called the Chixulub Basin in Mexico, lies partly beneath the sea and is 300 km across. It must have been made by a very large object, such as an asteroid, smashing into the Earth. Such a collision would have caused great changes to the climate, and so altered conditions for life on Earth. Every 50 million years, an asteroid measuring more than 10 km across hits the Earth.

➡ A comet that appeared in 1064 (probably Halley's) is shown in the Bayeux Tapestry, which tells the story of the Normandy Invasion of Britain in 1066.

Halley's **Comet**

1682 British astronomer Edmund Halley saw it and worked out that the comet (now named after him) would return in 76–77 years.

1759 Great excitement: the comet returned as predicted.

1835 The comet was seen, but was not so bright.

1910 Despite scientific progress, some superstitious people still feared that the reappearance of the comet heralded the end of the world.

1986 Several spacecraft flew close to the comet.

2062 The next time Halley's Comet will return.

Large meteorites to hit **Earth**

Name	Where	Weight
Hoba	Namibia	54 tonnes
Campo del Cielo	Argentina	41 tonnes
Ahnighito	Greenland	31 tonnes

Why not test your knowledge on the Universe! Try answering these questions to find out how much you really know about the planets in our Solar System, the Sun, the Moon, stars, galaxies, space exploration and much more. Questions are grouped into the subject areas covered within the pages of this book. See how much you remember and discover how much more you can learn!

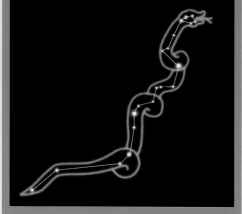

14 Is the constellation Hydra, the Water Snake, easy or difficult to spot in the night sky?

The Big Bang

1 How long ago is the Big Bang thought to have taken place?
2 Galaxies moved away from each other during the Big Bang. Do they still move today?
3 Did galaxies begin to form 3 million years, 30 million years or 300 million years after the Big Bang?

Stars

4 Stars are balls of hydrogen and which other gas?
5 Why do stars twinkle?
6 What do stars generate other than light?

Constellations

8 What kind of alphabet do astronomers use to list constellations?
9 How many constellations is the sky divided into?
10 Are there links between stars in constellations?

Galaxies

11 What is the name of the galaxy that Earth is in?
12 In which century did astronomers realize what galaxies consist of?
13 What shape is the Milky Way?

Far Away Objects

15 How long does it take light from the Sun to reach us on Earth?
16 The star Deneb is 1800 light-years away. Do we see it as it was at 20 BC, AD 20 or AD 200?
17 Which telescopes can detect matter further away from the Earth: light telescopes or radio telescopes?

Space Missions

18 Why don't astronauts float around in the spacecraft when they are asleep?
19 What earthly force acts against spacecrafts on take-off, and means that they must be equipped with rockets?
20 What did the first astronauts to land on the Moon bring back with them?

Searching the Sky

21 Why are observatories often built on mountain-tops?
22 Galileo gave his name to which planet's moons?
23 Who was the first astronomer to try to work out how far away the Sun is?

7 As comets orbit the Sun, they can form tails of up to how long: 100,000 km, 10 million km or 100 million km?

24 What passes directly in front of the Sun to create a solar eclipse?

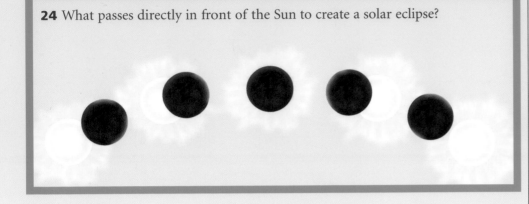

The Sun

25 How many times bigger is the Sun than the Earth: ten times, 100 times or 1,000 times?

26 What is the temperature of the Sun's surface?

27 Are sunspots hotter or cooler than the rest of the Sun's surface?

Earth in Space

28 How many planets away from the Sun is the Earth?

29 Has the Earth been formed over the last 4.5 million or 4.5 billion years?

30 Did volcanoes help to create the Earth's atmosphere?

The Moon

31 Approximately how long does it take the Moon to orbit the Earth: a day, a month or a year?

32 If a moon waxes, can we see more or less of it?

33 Is the gravity on the surface of the Moon more or less than on Earth?

Solar System

34 How many planets are in our Solar System?

35 Which planet is the smallest in our Solar System?

36 Which planet is nearest the Sun?

The Inner Planets

37 'The Evening Star' is another name for which planet?

38 How many moons does Mars have?

39 Which is hotter: Venus or Mercury?

The Outer Planets

40 Which planet is the biggest in our Solar System?

41 How long does Saturn take to travel around the Sun: two years, 20 years or 29 years?

42 Who was the first person to see Saturn's rings?

Rocks in Space

43 What are comets made of?

44 Who predicted that a comet would return in 1758, 16 years after his death?

45 Which star do most asteroids orbit?

Answers

1 15 billion years ago
2 Yes
3 300 million years
4 Helium
5 Because we see them through the Earth's atmosphere
6 Heat
7 100 million km
8 Greek
9 88
10 No, they are simply patterns
11 Milky Way

12 20th century
13 Spiral shaped
14 Difficult, because it is very dim
15 Eight minutes
16 AD 200
17 Radio telescopes
18 They are held in place by special stirrups
19 Gravity
20 Moon rock
21 So that city lights cannot interfere with the astronomers' vision

22 Jupiter
23 Hipparchus
24 The Moon
25 100 times
26 6,000°C
27 Cooler
28 Three
29 4.5 billion years
30 Yes
31 A month
32 More
33 Less

34 Nine
35 Pluto
36 Mercury
37 Venus
38 Two
39 Venus
40 Jupiter
41 29 years
42 Galileo
43 Ice
44 Halley
45 The Sun

Page numbers in **bold** refer to main subjects; page numbers in *italics* refer to illustrations.

The publishers would like to thank the following artists who have contributed to this book:
Vanessa Card, Kuo Kang Chen, Alan Hancocks, Rob Jakeway, Maltings, Janos Marffy, Andrea Morandi,
Martin Sanders, Peter Sarson, Mike Saunders, Rudi Vizi, Mike White

All photographs are from:
NASA, PhotoDisc